JARED MEEKER'S
Serious Shred

GET YOUR FINGERS TO PLAY
WHAT'S IN YOUR HEAD

Alfred Music Publishing Co., Inc.
P.O. Box 10003
Van Nuys, CA 91410-0003
alfred.com

ISBN-10: 0-7390-8608-1 (Book & DVD)
ISBN-13: 978-0-7390-8608-7 (Book & DVD)

Cover guitar courtesy of Jackson® Guitars, USA
Author photo courtesy of Jared Meeker

 Alfred Cares. Contents printed on 100% recycled paper.

Contents

TUNE UP

In the DVD menu, select Tuning. It will take you to a page where you will hear an audio track that will play each string several times, starting with the 1st string, high E. Compare your strings to this audio track to get in tune with the DVD.

A NOTE ABOUT THE VIDEO

The DVD video corresponds to lessons in the book and the two are intended to be used together. For lessons that use Jam Tracks, go to the DVD menu and select Jam Tracks, where you can access the tracks that correspond with specific lessons. The video lessons included on this DVD were filmed at various times over the period of a year; thus, you will note wardrobe and lighting changes from lesson to lesson.

Introduction

If you have been playing long enough to feel limited by what you know and what your fingers can do, the Serious Shred DVDs and books are for you. You have developed some lead guitar chops and know some scales and lots of chords, but would like to be able to play like the killer shredders you have heard. Each DVD/book combination in this series features a monster shredder guitarist teaching the left- and/or right-hand techniques and musical concepts you need to master to become the shredder you want to be. You'll be learning from the best, and will be inspired by the amazing demonstrations of licks and exercises in the video.

The optimum learning experience with the Serious Shred DVD/book series is to watch the video, guitar in hand ready to play, with the book open in front of you. Numbers will be displayed on your television or computer screen, directing you to licks, and exercises in the book that include standard music notation, TAB, and chord or scale fretboard diagrams. Stop the video any time you need to practice an example. Make sure you have mastered each lick or exercise before continuing to the next lesson will ensure the effectiveness of the training offered here.

To make it easier for you to select and use a Serious Shred DVD and book, they have been categorized into levels, which are explained below.

ESSENTIAL
This level assumes you can read TAB and/or standard music notation, and know how to read chord and scale fretboard diagrams. You know all of the basic open-position chords and are ready for barres and other movable chords. You have some familiarity with the pentatonic scale, and are ready to learn a number of alternate positions in which it can be played. You're ready to master the fundamental techniques, such as hammer-ons, pull-offs, alternate picking, and even some more specialized techniques, such as palm muting, bending, legato, vibrato, fingerstyle, tapping, and sweep picking. You have the theory background needed to begin learning the modes of the major scale, and putting them to use in solos.

ADVANCED
This level assumes you have all of the skills and knowledge developed at the ESSENTIAL level, and are ready to explore more advanced techniques and concepts. You have the musical understanding needed to learn all the different types of 7th chords, plus extended and altered chords in a variety of voicings. You're ready for advanced applications of sweeping, tapping, harmonics, and whammy bar techniques. You're ready to explore topics such as phrasing, multi-finger tapping, Hendrix-style chord embellishments, and more.

ABOUT JARED MEEKER

Jared Meeker is a versatile guitarist with experience in a variety of musical genres and styles. With endorsements by Line 6, Propellerhead, and Spalt Instruments, Jared is an accomplished, innovative musician, composer, producer, and performer in the Los Angeles area. He tours with Salvador Santana and is a music software test pilot for Propellerhead. In addition, Jared is also on faculty at Antelope Valley College and National Guitar Workshop, and owns and directs Spiderfingers Music Academy.

Comparing the Major Scale to the Mixolydian Mode

In our first lesson, we'll be discussing modes. The concept of modes is often misunderstood, so we'll clear up any misconceptions by introducing and comparing two of them: the major scale (which is the first mode, also called the *Ionian* mode) and the *Mixolydian* mode. What are modes? For now, we'll just think of them as scales. We'll talk more about that and get into the formulas that organize these scales and modes. But before we do, let's analyze two scales parallel to each other, built from the same root, and see how they differ.

THE MAJOR SCALE

The formula for the major scale, in terms of whole steps and half steps, is: whole–whole–half–whole–whole–whole–half. Let's try playing this on the A string.

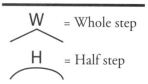

A Major Scale on One String

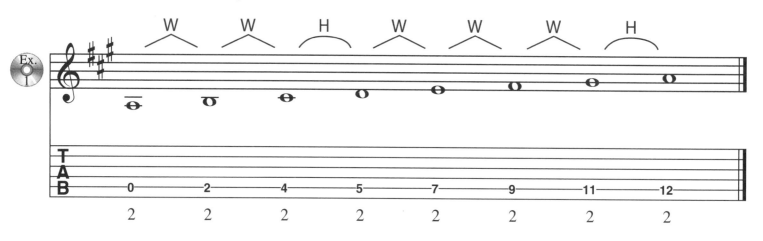

Now, let's learn a practical shape for the major scale that moves vertically across all six strings.

The cool thing about the scale above is that the string shapes are in pairs (5-7-9, 5-7-9; 6-7-9, 6-7-9, etc.), so it's relatively easy to visualize. Play the scale up and down until it feels comfortable.

A Major to G Major

Let's move the major scale around a bit to get comfortable with it. This next example changes from A Major to G Major. Off of each root (A and G), we will play the scale up to the 9th and back.

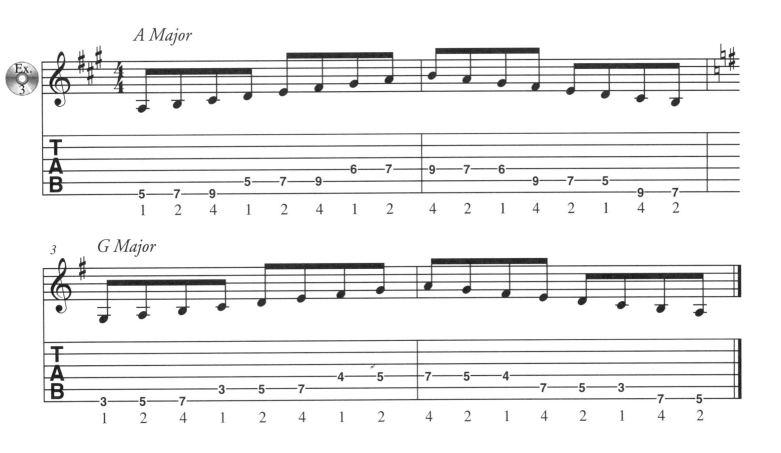

Now, let's move up one octave and do the same thing—play the A Major scale up nine notes and back, then move down two frets and do the same thing in G Major.

THE MIXOLYDIAN MODE

Let's check out the Mixolydian mode, which has a different formula of whole steps and half steps from the major scale. Its formula is: whole–whole–half–whole–whole–half–whole. On the A string, the Mixolydian mode would be played as follows.

A Mixolydian on One String

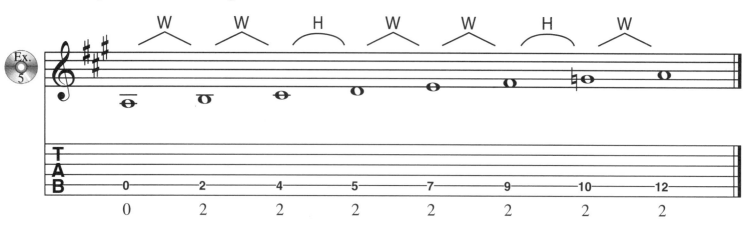

Check this out: Each note of a scale can be referred to as a number, or *scale degree.* If you look at the seven notes of the major scale as 1–2–3–4–5–6–7, then the Mixolydian, by comparison, would be 1–2–3–4–5–6–♭7. The only difference is that last note.

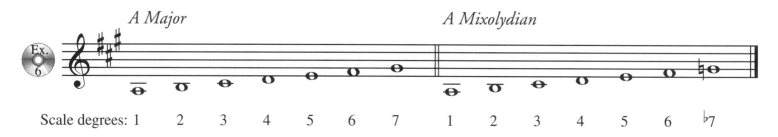

The type of chord that corresponds to the Mixolydian mode is a dominant chord, which is denoted by a letter followed by a 7 (A7, D7, F♯7, etc.). A G7 chord has a ♭7, just like G Mixolydian.

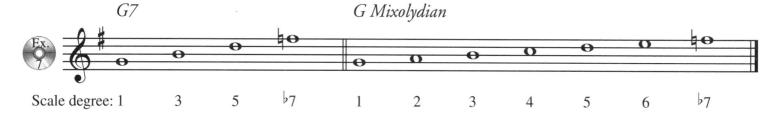

Let's learn the Mixolydian mode across all six strings. Since you already know the major scale, all you need to do is alter the 7's to ♭7's. Here we go.

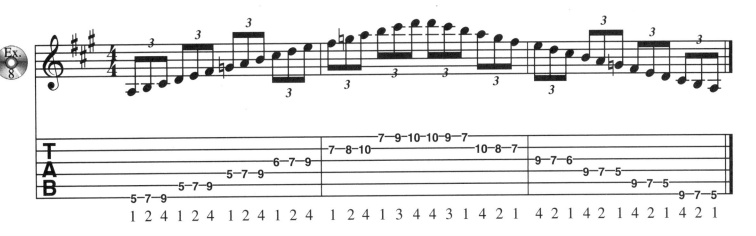

Now, we'll do the same exercises with the Mixolydian mode that we did with the major scale. Starting out on the 6th-string A note, play up nine notes of the Mixolydian mode and then come back down. Then do the same thing two frets lower in G Mixolydian.

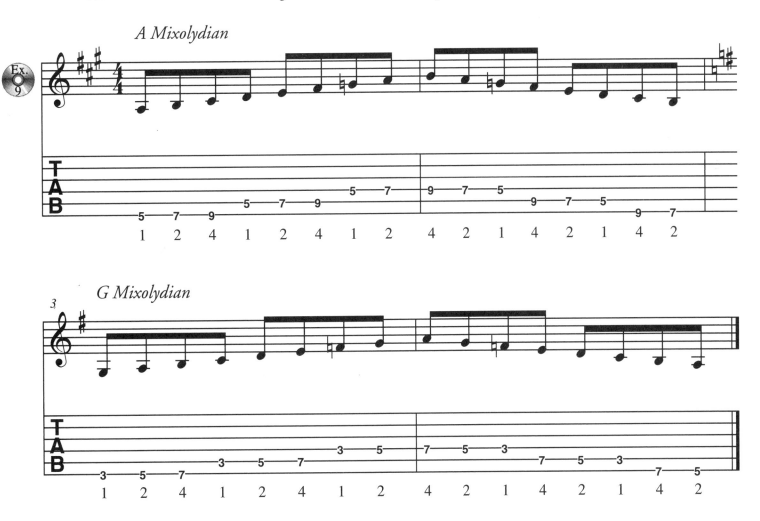

Let's do the same thing we did in the previous example, but one octave higher.

A Mixolydian

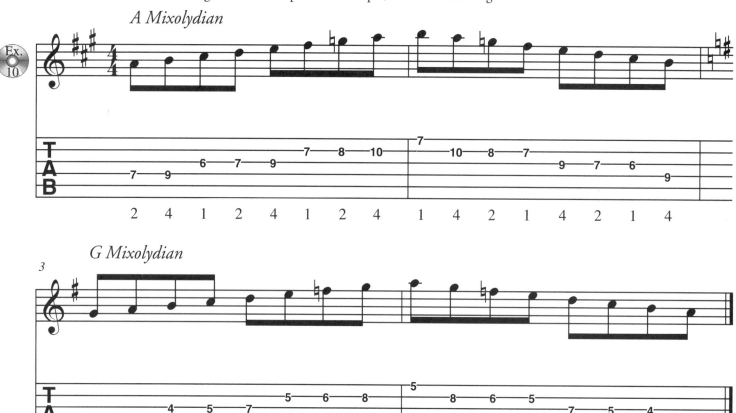

COMBINING THE MAJOR SCALE AND MIXOLYDIAN MODE

Now that you have both the major scale and Mixolydian shapes down pretty well, let's combine them. Starting on the 6th string, we'll ascend C Major for one octave, then descend from the 9th note of B Mixolydian, then ascend B♭ Major, and then descend A Mixolydian from the 9th note. Let's try it.

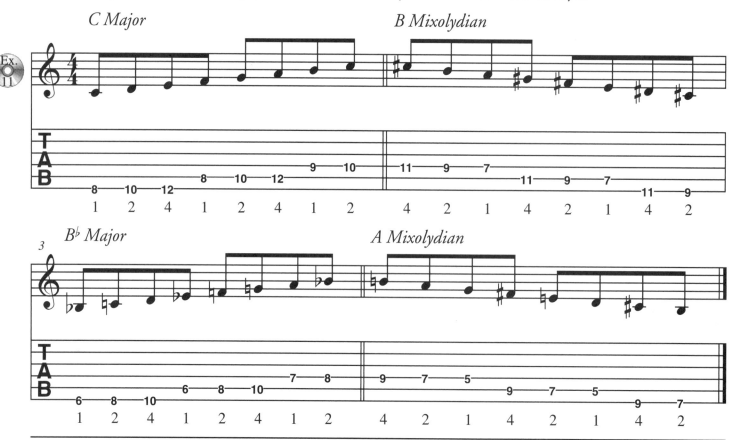

Great! Now, we'll do the same thing one octave higher. Ascend C Ionian, descend B Mixolydian, ascend B♭ Ionian, and descend A Mixolydian.

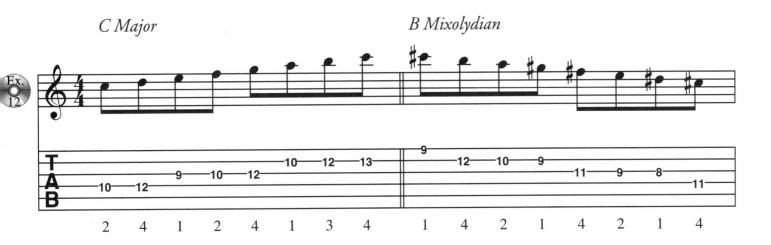

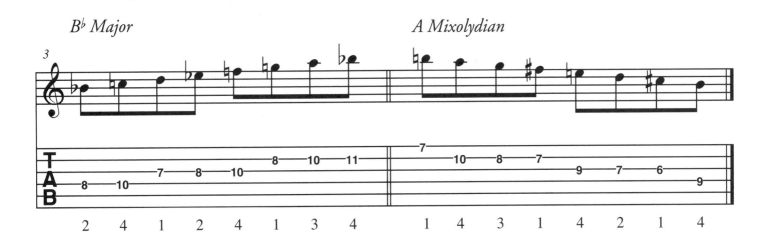

The last thing we need to do is play the full scale patterns (all six strings) through these same changes. Ascend C Major, descend B Mixolydian, ascend B♭ Major, and descend A Mixolydian.

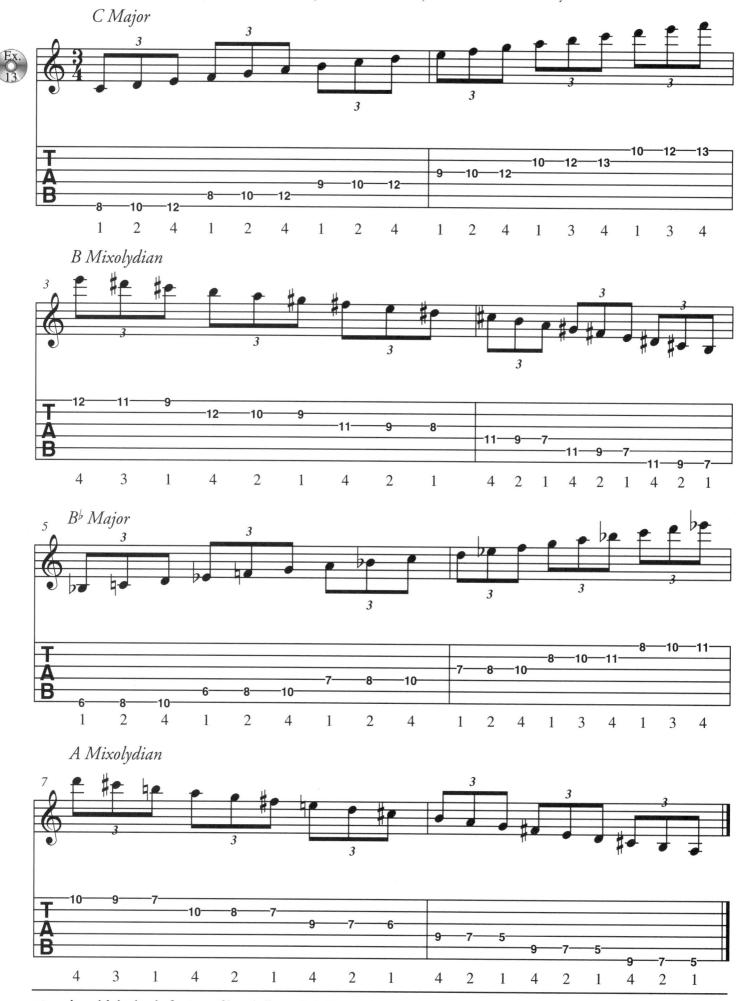

Expanded Fingerings for the Ionian and Mixolydian Modes

In the previous chapter, we covered the basic concept of how the major scale and Mixolydian mode differ from each other. Now, we'll look at how they are the same. In this lesson, you will learn how these two shapes are extended fingerings for the same seven notes. Then, we'll expand those fingerings into diagonal shapes, which are very useful for improvising.

THE DERIVATIVE CONCEPT OF MODES

In the last chapter, we used the *parallel* concept of comparing scales (starting different scales from the same root). Now, let's get into the *derivative* concept.

Modes are essentially just scale inversions. For instance, an A Major scale has seven notes (A–B–C♯–D–E–F♯–G♯) and, therefore, seven modes. If you play those notes starting on A, you're playing mode number one. If you play those same seven notes starting on B, that is mode number two, etc. Every mode has a Greek name. Ionian is mode number one. It is exactly the same as the major scale, so from here on out, we will refer to the major scale as Ionian. Mixolydian is mode number five.

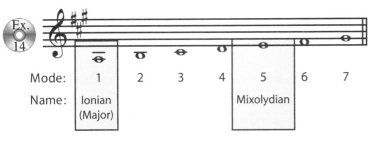

Mode:	1	2	3	4	5	6	7
Name:	Ionian (Major)				Mixolydian		

Note that A Ionian begins with the 1st note of the major scale and E Mixolydian starts with the 5th. Let's check out the spelling of these two modes. A Ionian is A–B–C♯–D–E–F♯–G♯, and E Mixolydian is E–F♯–G♯–A–B–C♯–D. They both have the same seven notes. (Note: The octave of the root note is played at the end of the scales for a sense of completion.)

A Ionian

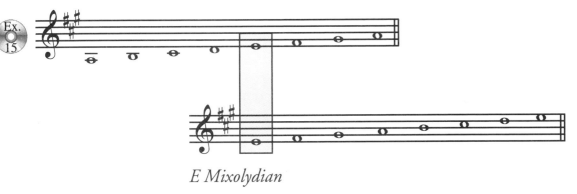

E Mixolydian

Now, let's play these modes on the guitar.

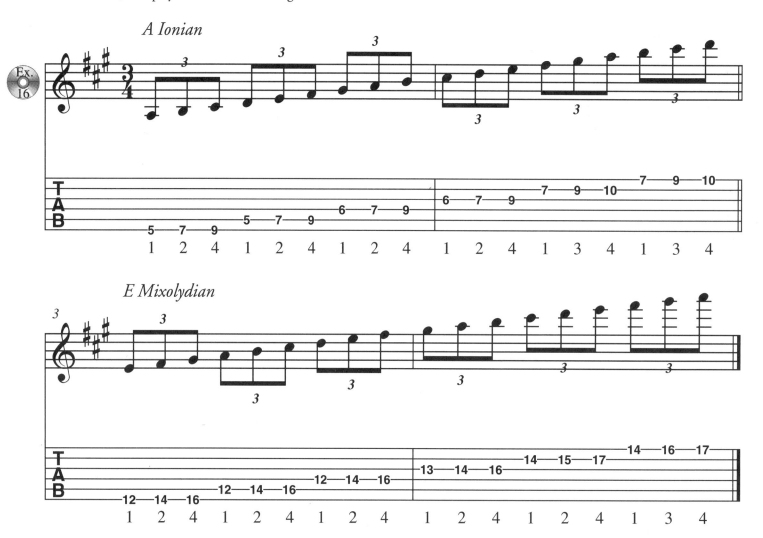

USING SCALE PATTERNS

So if your band says, "Dude, we've got this song that needs a solo—it's in G Major," you could easily find these shapes. First, where is G on the 6th string? 3rd fret, right? So, you play the major scale, or what we now call Ionian, starting at the 3rd fret of the 6th string. The next shape you could use is the Mixolydian mode off of the 5th degree—D on the 10th fret of the 6th string. Finally, to cover the entire fretboard, you can play G Ionian an octave higher from where you started, up at the 15th fret.

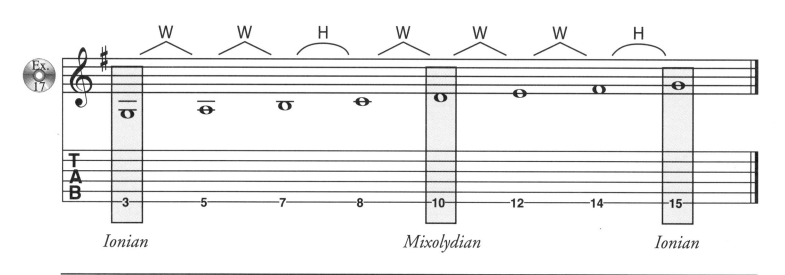

Following are all three shapes on the guitar.

G Ionian

D Mixolydian

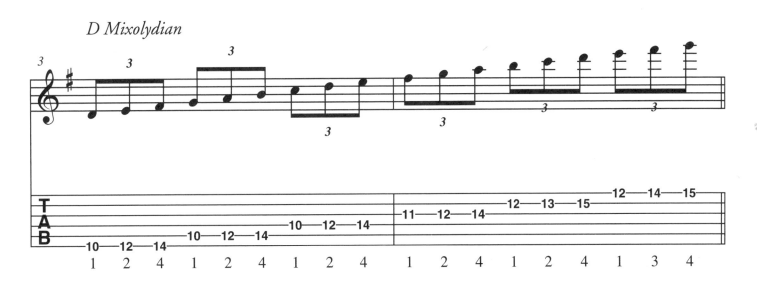

G Ionian

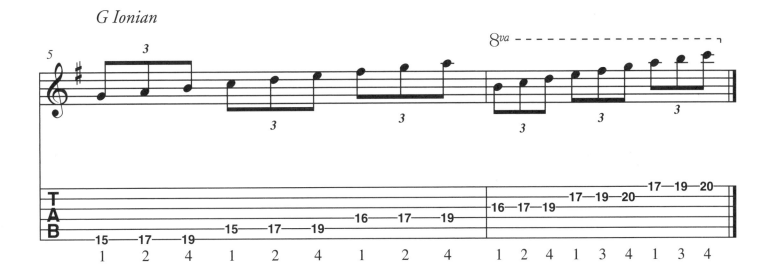

Now, you can use the entire neck for constructing your solo with just two simple shapes.

MIXOLYDIAN IN CONTEXT

You have already learned that Mixolydian is the 5th mode in a major key. Just as there is a different scale built off of each note of the major scale, there is also a different chord built off of each note. The fifth chord of the key is dominant in quality. Therefore, Mixolydian can be defined as a dominant scale. Dominant chords can sometimes be tricky to identify. For example, you rarely, if ever, see a chord labeled as "G Dominant"—it would be written as G7, G9, or even G13.

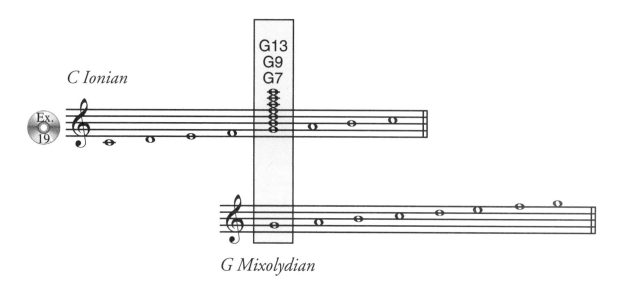

Dominant chords are an important part of harmony. For example, blues and funk musicians commonly *vamp* on dominant chords. (To "vamp" is to play a groove, or rhythm, using only one or two chords.) If you're playing on a tune that grooves on G7, you can easily apply the Ionian and Mixolydian modes. G Mixolydian starts at the 3rd fret of the 6th string, C Ionian starts at the 8th fret, and G Mixolydian, again, starts at the 15th fret.

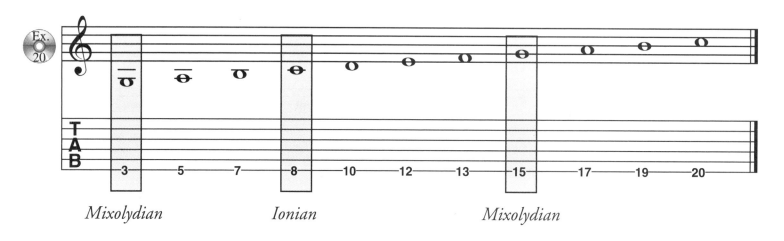

Following are all three shapes on the guitar.

G Mixolydian

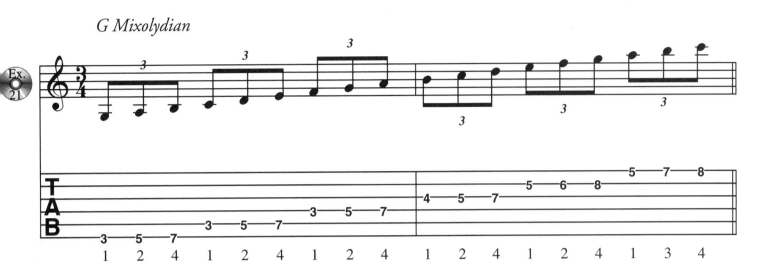

C Ionian

G Mixolydian

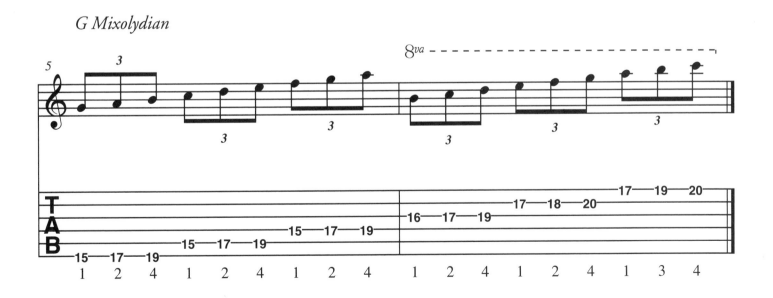

Diagonal Scale Patterns

In order to truly master the fretboard, it is essential to delve into diagonal shapes. First, here is G Ionian played diagonally across the neck.

G Ionian—Diagonal Pattern

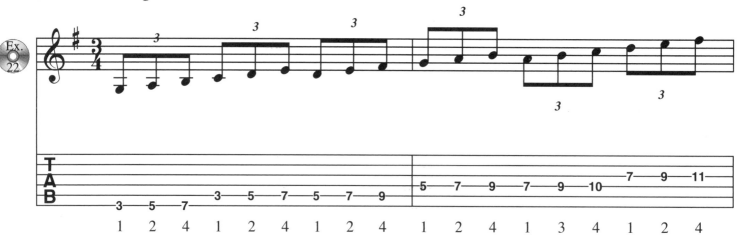

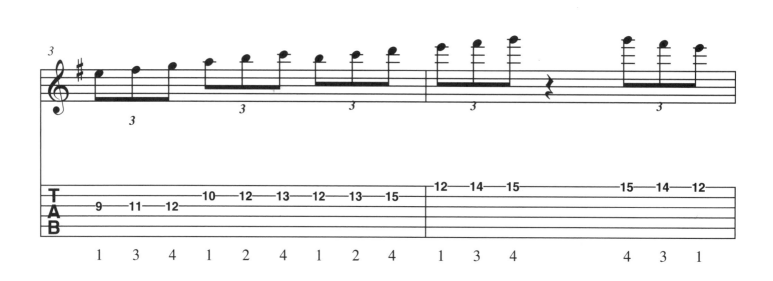

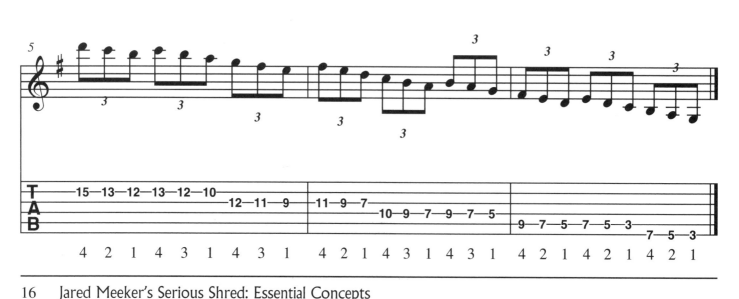

Next is G Mixolydian played diagonally.

G Mixolydian—Diagonal Pattern

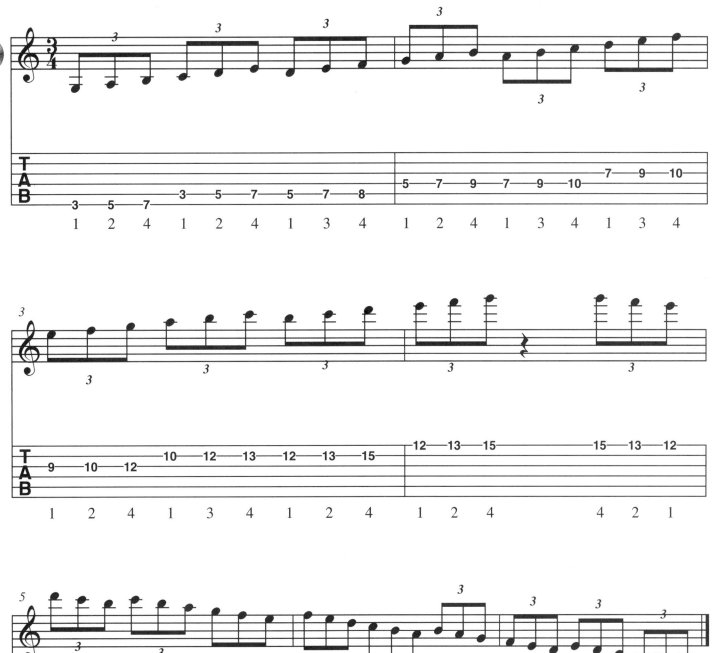

These sounds will allow you to explore the fretboard in new ways. We've only looked at two modes, but if you know how to apply them, you can use them in almost any context.

Using the Ionian and Mixolydian Modes in Musical Context

So, you've learned the Ionian and Mixolydian shapes—now, let's put that knowledge to use. I am going to show you six licks, and each will be played in different positions utilizing these two shapes. The phrases are divided into two categories: *comma* and *period*. Music is a language and can be phrased similar to speech and writing. Commas are used for dramatic effect, to pause your idea before concluding your statement. Periods are used for a feeling of finality or resolution. Musically, we will just say that period phrases end on the root note and comma phrases do not. You will understand this more as we play along with the G7 vamp on the video. What you need to do is repeat musical phrases over and over until they become a part of your musical vocabulary and you can speak the language.

COMMA PHRASES

First, we'll look at comma phrases. The real areas of melodic tension and resolution are in the half-step movements of the scale. The following example locates the half steps in different registers of the instrument. Notice that I'm playing in four registers: two within the shape of G Mixolydian and two within the Ionian shape at the 8th fret.

More Comma Phrases

Okay, let's move on to the next example. We'll use the same concept, but we are going to play two registers in the Mixolydian shape and one in the Ionian.

All the comma phrases we have looked at are *syncopated* (the emphasis is placed on parts of the beat not usually emphasized), so make sure your rhythms are tight. Loop each riff over and over until it becomes a part of your vocabulary. Below is our final comma phrase.

Now, practice all the comma phrases we have worked on, and try playing them along with the jam track on the DVD.

PERIOD PHRASES

Let's move on to period phrases, or licks that end on our root note (in this case, G).

Notice that period phrases have a bit more resolution than comma phrases. Check out the next example.

Below is our final period phrase of this lesson.

Improvising Using the Ionian and Mixolydian Modes

You can develop your improvisation skills by combining previously composed material and spur of the moment improvisation. In this chapter, using the licks from previous lessons, we will combine comma and period phrases so you can communicate musical statements.

CALL AND RESPONSE

Call and response is a musical technique where a statement is made by one phrase and is answered by another. In this section, I will lead you into a call and response where I play the comma phrase (the call) and you play the period phrase (the response). You may respond with any phrase in any register that we worked on in the last chapter. Use the example below to prepare your responses, then play along with the DVD.

(Continued on next page)

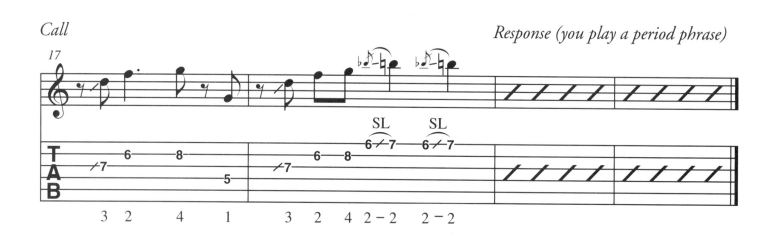

Good! Now, let's do the opposite. I'll play the period phrase, and you answer me with one of the comma phrases in any register.

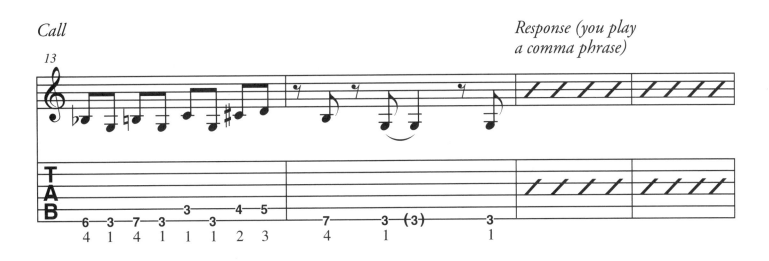

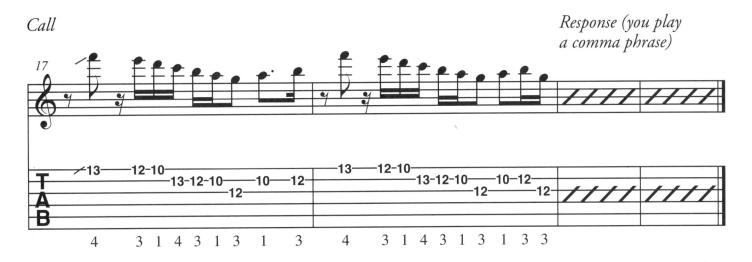

COMBINING COMMA AND PERIOD PHRASES

Now, it's time to solo on your own by alternating the various comma and period phrases.
Following is an example of how you can flip between one melody and the next to create a solo.
Check it out.

Try playing the example above with the jam track on the DVD, then experiment by combining other period and comma phrases.

USING A COMMA PHRASE AND IMPROVISING

In the next exercise, we will alternate between one comma phrase and two measures of an improvised period phrase. Make sure to watch the DVD for an example of how to do this. If you have a hard time coming up with ideas, try altering the phrases you've already learned. You can take this as far out as you want, but remember to resolve your period phrases on the root note G.

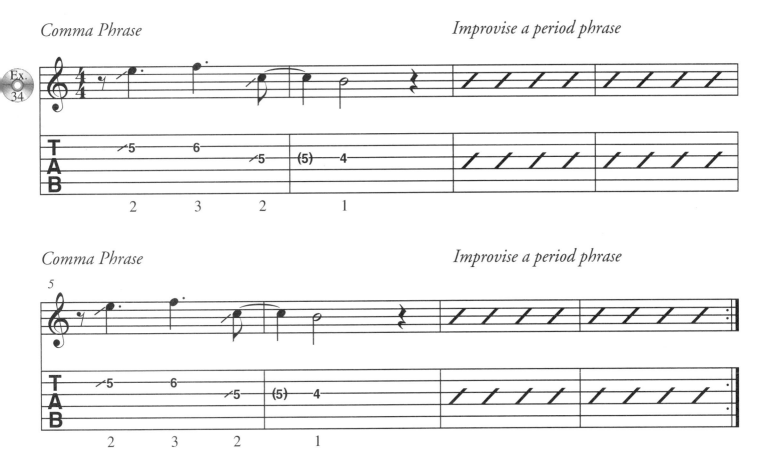

Now, it's your turn! Play along with the jam track on the DVD and try alternating comma phrases with improvised period phrases.

This lesson will sharpen your improvisation skills. The comma/period concept will help give shape and movement to your solos. Develop some of your own ideas and listen to what naturally comes out of your head and hands.

Fingerstyle

Fingerstyle often gets the cold shoulder in the rock arena. In this lesson, we are going to step away from sweep picking, arpeggios, and tapping, and look at how we can use fingerstyle technique to add more depth to our playing.

THREE-NOTE ROLLS

Let's take a basic three-finger roll and apply it to a basic three-note chord, the triad. An important part of music theory is understanding *diatonic harmony,* or the chords within a key. A chord can be built on each note of the major scale, and each of those chords has a particular *quality* (major, minor, or diminished). There's a specific formula for the chords in a major key, and it goes like this: major–minor–minor–major–major–minor–diminished. Check out the example below for an illustration of this concept in the key of C Major.

Diatonic Triads in the Key of C Major

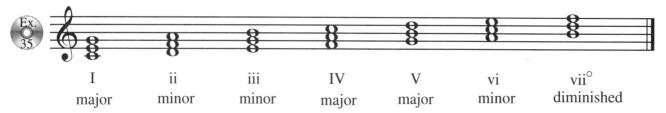

I	ii	iii	IV	V	vi	vii°
major	minor	minor	major	major	minor	diminished

Let's talk for just a moment about the right hand. The guitar originated in Spain, so the symbols indicating the right-hand fingers represent Spanish terms: *p* is for *pulgar* (thumb), *i* for *indice* (index finger), *m* for *medio* (middle finger), and *a* for *anular* (ring finger).

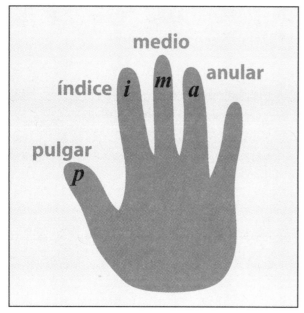

In our first example, which is in the key of B Major, you will play each triad two times with a basic *p-i-m* fingerpicking pattern. (Note: *simile* means continue in the same style.)

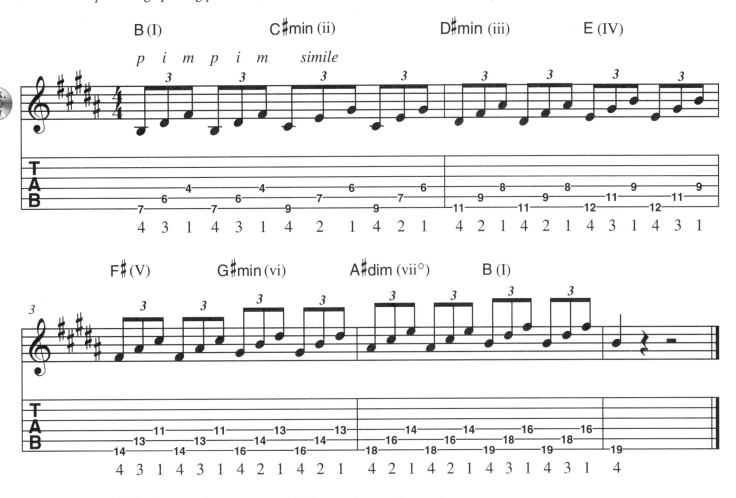

Next, we'll do the same thing one octave higher on the top three strings.

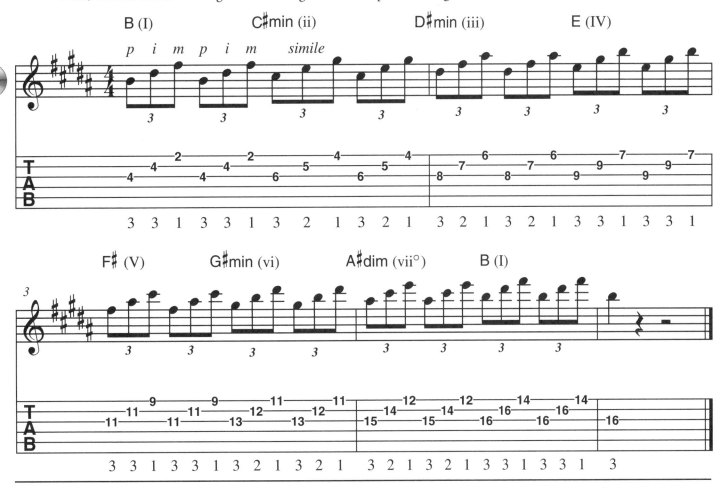

BACKWARD THREE-NOTE ROLLS

Chords can also be built on each note of the natural minor scale. A minor key has a different chord formula than a major key, and it is: minor–diminished–major–minor–minor–major–major.

Diatonic Triads in the Key of A Minor

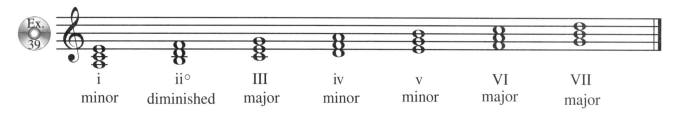

The next two licks are backward rolls through B Minor. For these, you will fingerpick *m-i-p*.

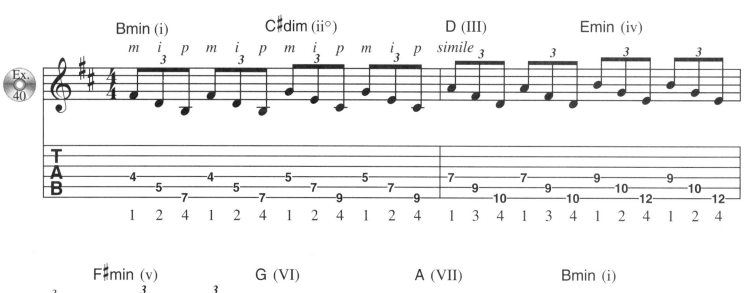

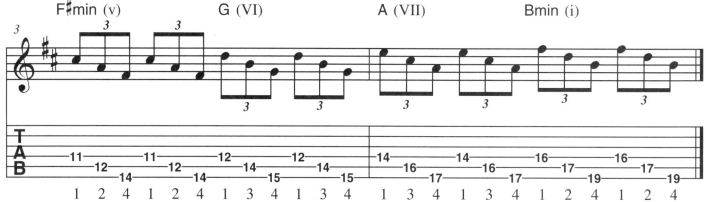

Now, let's take the backward rolls up one octave to the top three strings.

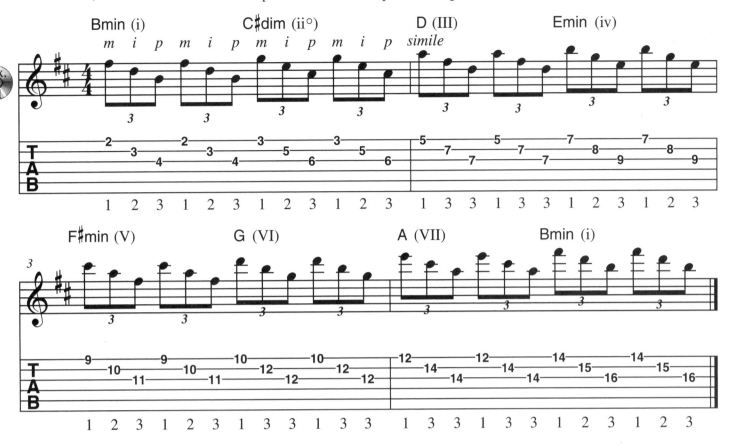

CONNECTING THREE-STRING ARPEGGIOS

Let's take the concept we've been working on across the strings with an arpeggio sequence of threes. The following example ascends an E Major triad at the 7th fret, descends a B♭ Major triad at the 13th fret, ascends another E triad an octave higher at the 19th fret, comes back down the B♭ Major arpeggio, and ends on E. Check it out.

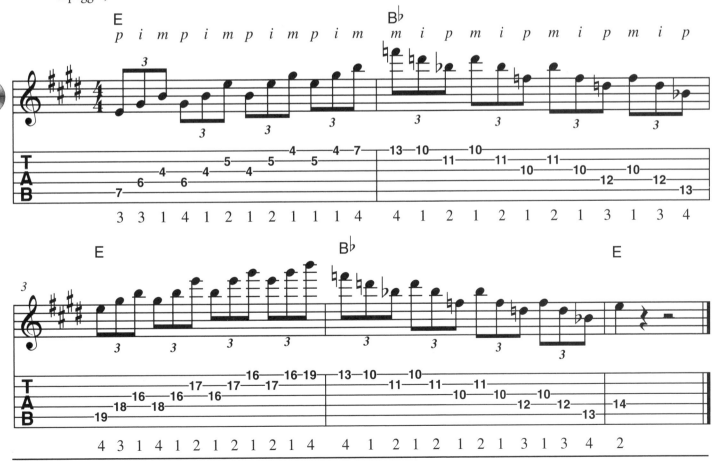

Pattern Playing: Lesson 1

In this lesson, we are going to learn about *pattern* playing, or *sequencing,* which is the repetition of a musical phrase at various pitch levels. We'll be using leaps, intervals, arpeggios, and pedal licks to create some interesting patterns. All of the examples in this lesson use the A Major scale in the three-note-per-string fingering (see right). The following ideas will expand your musical knowledge and develop your improvisational skills.

A Major Scale Fingering for This Lesson (Three Notes Per String)

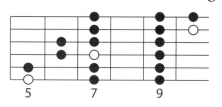

THREE-NOTE PATTERN

We will start by playing the A Major scale in the following pattern: three notes up, back one, three notes up, and back one. The numeric sequence for this pattern, in term of scale degrees, is: 1-2-3, 2-3-4, 3-4-5, etc. Check it out.

Scale degree: 1 2 3 2 3 4 etc.

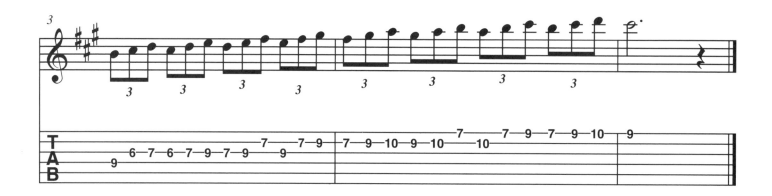

We can also play the above pattern in reverse: 3-2-1, 4-3-2, 5-4-3, etc. The fingering for Ex. 45 is tricky—use whatever fingering is most logical to you. (Note: You may choose to flatten your fretting finger when changing strings at the same fret.)

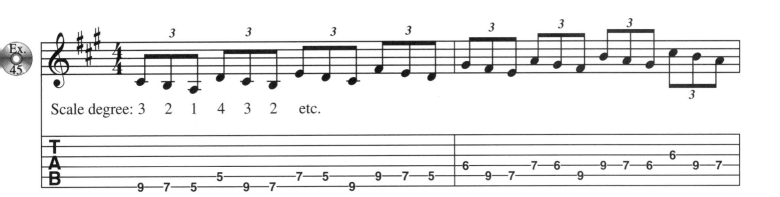

Scale degree: 3   2   1   4   3   2   etc.

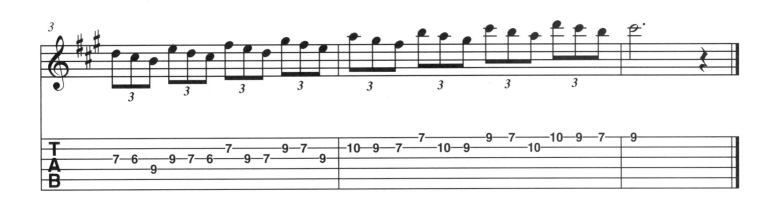

EXPANDING THE PATTERN

Next, let's flip the pattern each time. First, you will play three as normal, 1-2-3, then backwards, 4-3-2, then 3-4-5, 6-5-4, 5-6-7, 8-7-6, etc. Check out the following example.

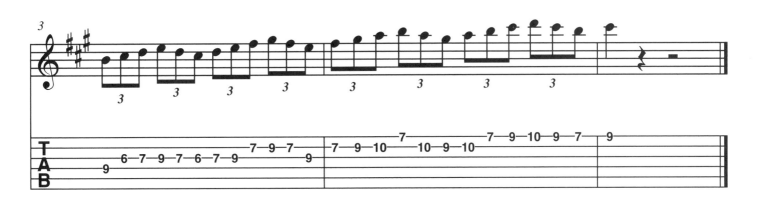

Scale degree: 1   2   3   4   3   2   etc.

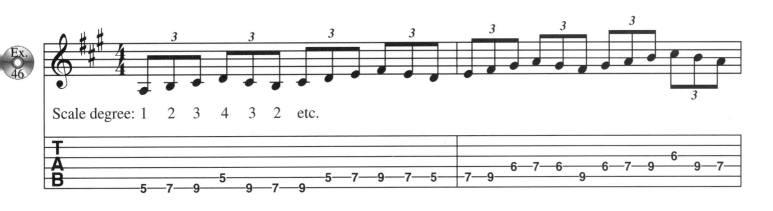

You can do these kinds of licks with two-note patterns, four-note patterns, five-note patterns, etc.—the possibilities are endless.

Let's try an example with a four-note pattern: 1-2-3-4, 2-3-4-5, 3-4-5-6, 4-5-6-7, 5-6-7-8, etc.

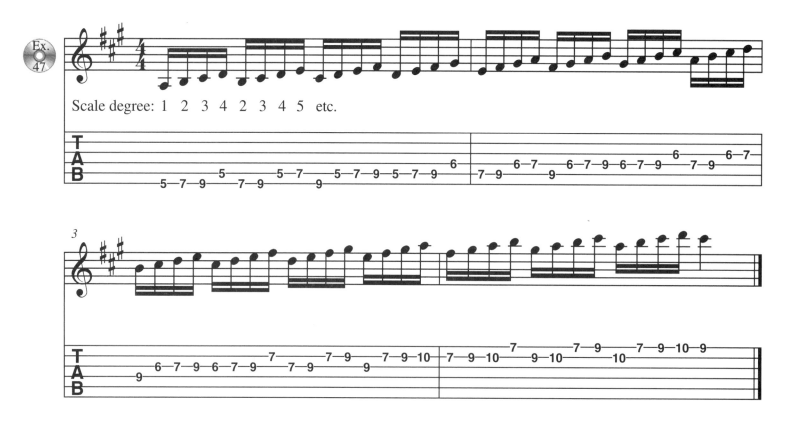

Now, let's do the *retrograde* of the above example. Retrograde is a pattern played backwards, so this one would be: 4-3-2-1, 5-4-3-2, 6-5-4-3, 7-6-5-4, 8-7-6-5, etc.

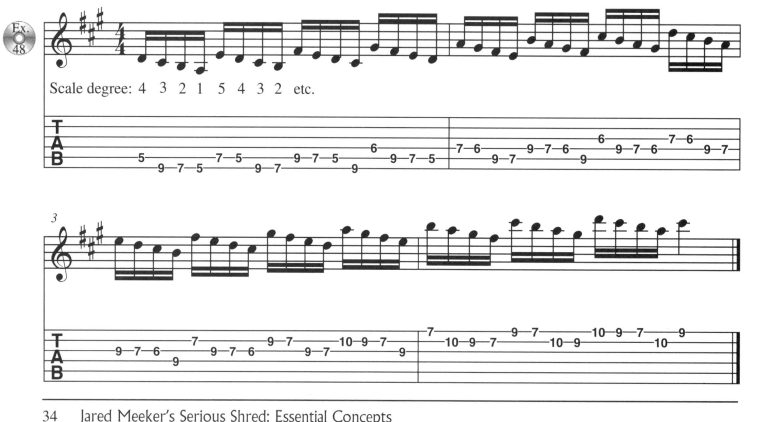

Finally, we'll alternate between ascending and descending forms: 1-2-3-4, 5-4-3-2, etc.

Scale degree: 1 2 3 4 5 4 3 2 etc.

INTERVAL LEAPS

There are many intervals you can use to leap through a scale. First, let's do this with 3rds. The numeric sequence would be: 1-3, 2-4, 3-5, 4-6, 5-7, 6-8, etc.

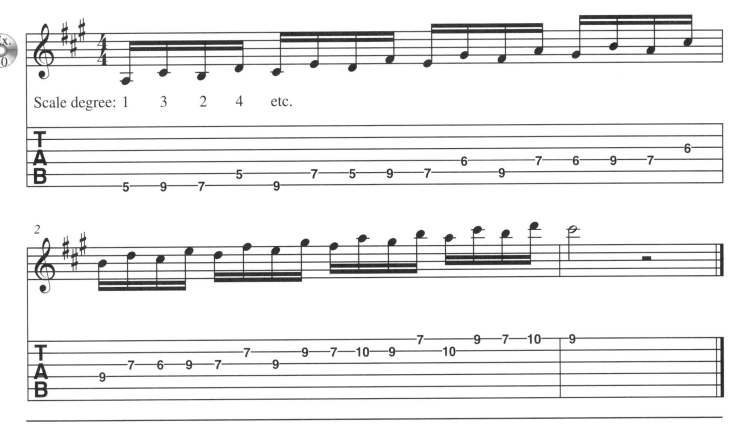

Scale degree: 1 3 2 4 etc.

Now, let's try 6ths: 1-6, 2-7, 3-8, 4-9, etc.

Scale degree: 1   6   2   7   etc.

Remember, you can ascend or descend these patterns, and you can also alternate between the two.

ARPEGGIOS

Now, let's combine leaps to form *arpeggios*. An arpeggio is the notes of a chord played separately, rather than simultaneously. Triads are formed with scale degrees 1-3-5. Let's move that pattern up the scale so we have: 1-3-5, 2-4-6, 3-5-7, 4-6-8, 5-7-9, 6-8-10, etc.

Scale degree: 1   3   5   2   4   6   etc.

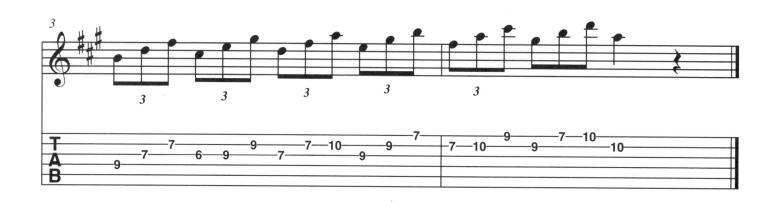

Now, let's alternate ascending and descending arpeggios: up 1-3-5, down 6-4-2, up 3-5-7, down 8-6-4, etc.

Scale degree: 1   3   5   6   4   2   etc.

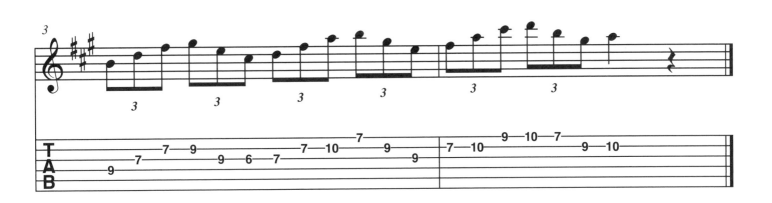

PEDAL LICK

A *pedal tone* is a note repeated over and over while melodies or harmonies change above or below it. The pedal tone is used as a pivot in a pattern. Our pedal lick is as follows: 1-3, 1-4, 1-5, 1-6; 2-4, 2-5, 2-6, 2-7; 3-5, 3-6, 3-7, 3-8, etc.

Scale degree: 1   3   1   4   1   5   1   6   2   4   2   5   2   6   2   7   etc.

Okay, now you have plenty of ideas to work with. Imagine all these sequences applied to different scales: the harmonic minor scale, diminished scales, arpeggios, or even the pentatonic scale. The sky's the limit, so experiment and enjoy.

Pattern Playing: Lesson 2

Now, we're going to work on some advanced concepts that build on the previous pattern playing lesson (page 32). We'll explore moving lines by large intervals, taking patterns through leaps, and sequencing arpeggios. Then, we will also get into expansions, reductions, and combinations.

SEQUENCES MOVING IN INTERVALS

Let's break away from moving in 2nds and take wider leaps. We'll start by moving in 3rds with a four-note pattern: 1-2-3-4, 3-4-5-6, 5-6-7-8, 7-8-9-10, etc. This pattern works great because it accents the chord tones, or the 1-3-5-7, and then continues on through the extensions of tertian harmony. Check it out. (The A Minor scale being used is to the right, and the sequence is below.)

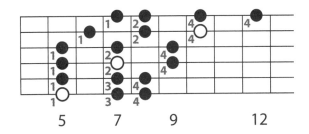

Sequence in 3rds

Next, let's use an interval of a 5th and move it around in 3rds through A Natural Minor. The number sequence is: 1-5, 3-7, 5-9, 7-11, etc.

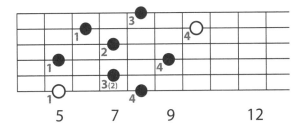

Sequence in 3rds (Using 5ths)

Finally, let's check out triads leaping in 4ths. This is a great interval for guitarists because the guitar is tuned almost entirely in 4ths. The following sequence is 1-3-5, 4-6-8, 7-9-11, etc.

Ascending

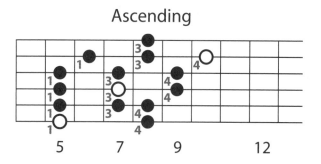

Descending

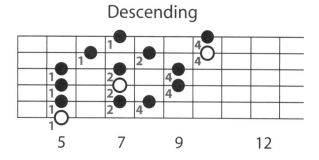

Triads Leaping in 4ths

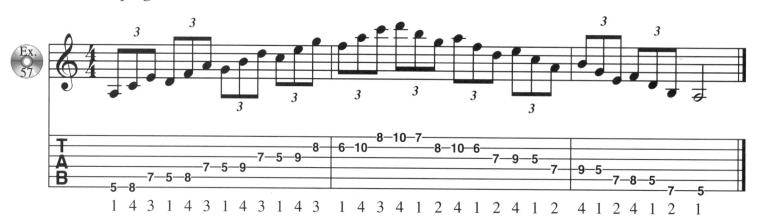

EXPANSION AND REDUCTION

An *expansion* is a type of sequence in which the phrase is added onto with each iteration, for example: 1-2, 1-2-3, 1-2-3-4, 1-2-3-4-5, 1-2-3-4-5-6, etc. You can do this in many different intervals, such as three notes at a time or four notes at a time. The concept has many possibilities and directions.

A *reduction* is the opposite; you take a longer phrase and tear away at it, like: 1-2-3-4-5-6, 1-2-3-4-5, 1-2-3-4, 1-2-3, 1-2.

To understand this topic better, we're going to play an A Natural Minor scale in one-note expansions until it gets to the 12th note, and then we'll do a reduction. Check it out.

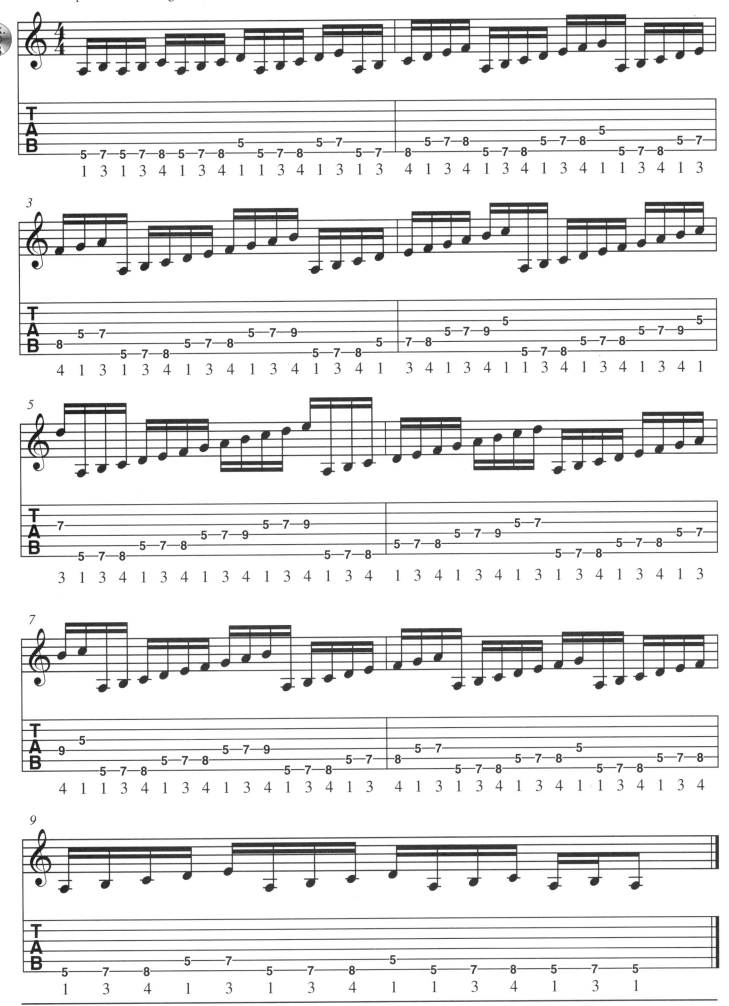

Applying Triads to a Three-Note Scale

There are so many ways of combining sequences that I could write an entire book on pattern combinations alone. However, we'll check out one great lick that combines triads with a scale sequence of threes. Here it is:

The possibilities with sequences are virtually endless. Try coming up with your own patterns and combinations of patterns. Use your ideas to develop your own unique sound.

Phrase Construction: Lesson 1

A musical *phrase* is a short segment of music that is usually part of a larger piece. The purpose of a phrase is to convey a musical idea or emotion. So, think of phrases as "samples"—little bits of information you can stream together to make a musical statement. The trick is in how your phrases relate to each other. If you have two phrases that are similar, then there won't be a tremendous impact on the listener. However, if you piece together phrases that contrast each other, then the listener will think, "Whoa! Where did that come from?" I'm going to show you how the concept of *duality* can transform your playing.

SOUND AND SILENCE

First of all, notation itself is comprised of a duality. We have symbols that represent sound, called notes, and symbols that represent silence, called rests. So, shredders, you need to take a break every once in a while. Trust me, it will let your playing breathe and will make it more effective.

Our first example alternates between sound for one measure and silence for the next. In your measure of sound, you can do anything—any kind of solo or rhythm will work. The only rule is that you have to stop at the beginning of the second and fourth measures. Play along with the jam track on the DVD and let your solo rip, keeping this idea in mind!

(Solo — — — — — Silence — — —) Solo — — — — — — — — Silence — — — —

*On the video, the author sits
out the first two measures.*

EXPANDING THE CONCEPT

Let's do the same thing across a four-bar phrase. This will give you more time for development. Practice this now, keeping the rhythm in mind as you play along with the jam track.

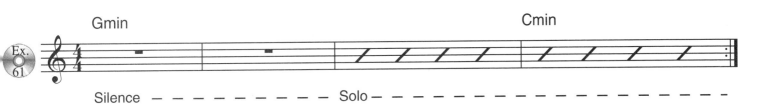

Silence — — — — — — — — Solo — — — — — — — — — — — — — —

DENSE AND SPARSE

The terms *dense* and *sparse* can mean many things, but for now, we'll look at dense as meaning many notes, and sparse as meaning very few notes. This is like the difference between sixteenth notes and half notes. The following is an exercise in note length, so play the entire time, but alternate between dense for one measure and sparse for the next. Play along with the jam track on the DVD.

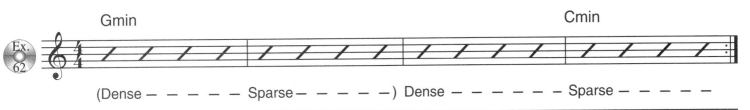

(Dense — — — — — Sparse — — — — —) Dense — — — — — — Sparse — — — — —

Once you have the dense and sparse concept down for two-bar phrases, you can always extend it to four-bar phrases. Try this along with the jam track.

(Sparse — — — — — — — — — — —) Dense — — — — — — — —

Up and Down

Up and down can be interpreted in many ways, but for now, it will mean high notes and low notes. So, in the next example, play on the treble strings (the thinnest, top three strings) for one measure, and then on the bass strings (the thickest, bottom three) for one measure. Repeat this, along with the jam track, until you are comfortable with the concept of up and down.

(Up — — — — — Down — — — — —) Up — — — — — — Down — — — — —

Next, let's apply up and down to a four-bar phrase.

(Down — — — — — — — — — — —) Up — — — — — — — — — — —

Play and Repeat

Play and repeat is one of the best exercises for an improviser. You play something new for one measure, and then repeat what you just did for the next measure. This forces you to listen to yourself as you improvise and respond to it. Check out my demonstration on the video, and then try it yourself to the jam track.

(Play — — — — - Repeat — — — — —) Play — — — — — - Repeat — — — —

Now, we're going to do the same thing for a four-bar phrase: two measures of new material and two measures of repeat. Again, check out the demonstration on the video, then try it along with the jam track.

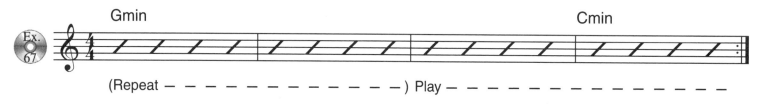

(Repeat — — — — — — — — — —) Play — — — — — — — — — — —

Hopefully, this lesson puts a breath of life into your playing and improvising. Make these ideas your own, and your soloing will take on a whole new dimension.

Phrase Construction: Lesson 2

It's time to explore another concept of phrasing. One very important part of standard, classical, and jazz theory is the concept of the non-harmonic tone. Have you ever heard about passing tones on strong and weak beats? These concepts about how melody relates to harmony have been around for hundreds of years and have survived for a reason—they just sound good.

OUTLINING THE CHORD

Let's look at a few phrasing techniques to help you outline the harmony and chord progressions under your solos. This could work for any chord, but for now, we're going to use Amin7. Below is an Amin7 arpeggio.

Amin7 Arpeggio

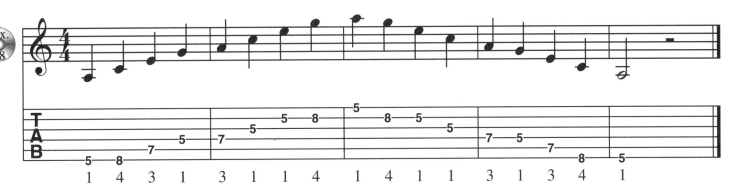

Next, let's outline the Amin7 arpeggio with *upper neighbor tones* (tones one half step above the chord tones). In other words, play the chord tone, move up a half step, and then back down. Check out the following example.

Applying Passing Tones

Another way to move between chord tones is by using *passing tones*. The most common passing tones are just scale tones that belong to the key in which you are playing, but a few alterations can be made to carve out the harmony a little better. I'm going to show you a trick. If you take a Dorian scale and add a natural 7th to it, you get eight notes to the octave—perfect for phrasing in $\frac{4}{4}$ time. Here's the scale.

A Dorian with Added Natural 7th

Now, let's play it.

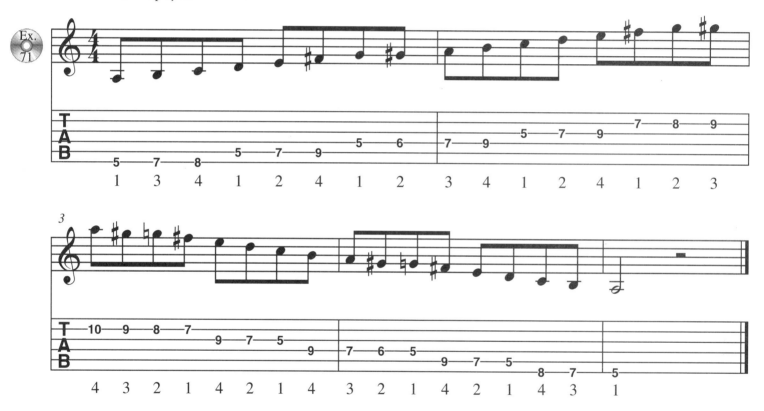

So what does this do? Well, first of all, it puts every other note on a chord tone. Check it out. When playing eighth notes, the metronome will click on your 1, ♭3, 5, and ♭7. This allows you to phrase around the harmony. If you begin on a downbeat, you start your phrase on a chord tone. If you begin your phrase on an upbeat, then your melody will start with a passing tone.

PHRASES BEGINNING ON DOWNBEATS AND UPBEATS

There are melodic strong beats and weak beats. The strong beats are basically the downbeats, or numbers (1, 2, 3, 4) and the weak beats are the upbeats, or "ands" (1-&, 2-&, 3-&, 4-&). How you start your line is very important, so, below, we'll practice starting on strong beats.

The following example, which starts on the downbeat, begins on the root of the chord and moves up four notes of the new Dorian scale, then goes to the next chord tone and continues the pattern. Check it out.

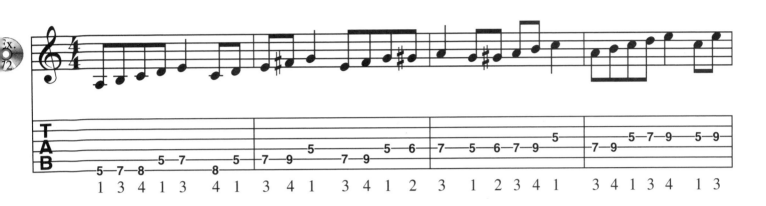

Now, we'll explore starting on a weak beat and go up an octave from each chord tone. Be sure to begin with an upstroke.

This idea of adding a natural 7th works great for any scale with a flat 7th and brings out its harmony. I encourage you to explore more non-harmonic tones.

CONGRATULATIONS!

You have completed *Jared Meeker's Serious Shred: Essential Concepts.* If you've been practicing and reading carefully, you have gained some important skills and knowledge. Be sure to check out the other DVD/book combos in the Serious Shred series.